Reflections
OF A
Thankful Heart

LORI WICK
paintings by DONNY FINLEY

HARVEST HOUSE PUBLISHERS
EUGENE, OREGON 97402

HARVEST HOUSE PUBLISHERS
EUGENE, OREGON 97402

I wish to dedicate this book to the countless people who have helped me

on my own journey to thankfulness. God bless you, one and all.

Lori

Reflections of a Thankful Heart

Text Copyright © 2000 by Lori Wick

Published by Harvest House Publishers

Eugene, Oregon 97402

Library of Congress Cataloging-in-Publication Data

Wick, Lori

    Reflections of a thankful heart/Lori Wick; paintings by Donny Finley.

       p. cm.

    ISBN 0-7369-0298-8 (hardcover)

    1. Christian life Meditations. I. Title.

    BV4501.2.w49 2000

    242--dc21   99-37263
                                   CIP

Artwork designs are reproduced under license from © Arts Uniq®, Inc., Cookeville, TN and may not be reproduced without permission. For information regarding art prints featured in this book, please contact:

    Arts Uniq'

    P.O. Box 3085

    Cookeville, TN 38502

    800-223-5020

Design and production by Koechel Peterson & Associates, Minneapolis, Minnesota

Unless indicated otherwise, Scripture quotations are from the King James Version. Verses marked NIV are from the Holy Bible, New International Version®. Copyright © 1973, 1978, 1984, by the International Bible Society. Used by permission of Zondervan Publishing House. Verses marked NASB are from the New American Standard Bible, © 1960, 1962, 1963, 1968, 1971, 1972, 1973, 1975, 1977 by The Lockman Foundation. Used by permission.

Printed in Hong Kong

00 01 02 03 04 05 06 07 08 09 / IM / 10 9 8 7 6 5 4 3 2 1

"The Mission" by Jon Mohr and Randall Dennis. Copyright © 1989 Sony/ATV Tunes LLC/Molto Bravo! Music. All rights administered by Sony/ATV Music Publishing, 8 Music Square West, Nashville, TN 37203. All Rights Reserved. Used by Permission.

Contents

Reflections of a Thankful Heart 4

Family 10

The Little Things 17

Girlfriends 20

Doors 25

Persistence 29

Christmas 34

Guys 39

Church Cleaning 44

Dad 49

Thorns 52

Living Water 56

Honesty 61

Reflections of a Thankful Heart

Every year we look forward to our hometown's annual Wild West Days celebration, which is always highlighted by a grand parade. This year's parade day was warm—a scorcher, in fact. As thermometers reached well above eighty degrees, the heat sent my family and me scrambling for the comfort of the shade long before the proud horses marched through at the end. Earlier, before the parade began, our household was in something of a frantic rush that only seemed to make the day warmer. One child had to be dropped off at the high school, where he would climb into uniform and march with the rest of the high school band, whereas our other student musician had to meet the rest of the middle school band at the car wash.

Trying to beat the clock, we quickly ate our lunch and managed to get everyone to the correct place at the correct time. When at last I blissfully sank into my comfy lawn chair along the parade route, water bottle close at hand, it occurred to me that our quick dashing around and seemingly packed schedule weren't such bad things. For my part in this parade, I needed only to make sure my two young men got to the right place at the right time, and I was blessed with a supportive husband to help me do it. I *could* have been in charge of something much bigger—say, one of the floats. I told my husband this, expressing that I was thankful to have had such a small role that day.

In all of life's varied circumstances, thankfulness is a choice we make each day, in each situation—big parade celebrations or small day-to-day responsibilities. There isn't a better way to say it. Thankfulness might not always look like someone skipping merrily along through life, smelling flowers without a care in the world, but possessing a thankful heart is nonetheless a tremendous asset. I like to call it an asset because of one of the ways the dictionary describes that word: *an item of value owned*. If you've ever made a choice to be thankful, you know just how true to life this definition is. A thankful heart is something of great value, and if you do own one, you're most likely smiling as you read this.

I was fairly young at the time, but I still recall watching an old Western that highlighted a jaded cowboy's life. I can't remember the whole storyline, but I can still imagine the campfire scene when the cowboy holds out his cup to a woman with a coffeepot. He's upset that she didn't give him more coffee. She looks into his cup and says it's still half-full. His gritty reply is that it's half-empty. For some odd reason, those two varying perspectives have always stayed in my memory.

I'm not a person who bases my faith on the power of positive thinking; that's not my point. But just like the woman holding the coffeepot, I didn't have to look very far to find something to be thankful about that day at the parade. Looking around at the hustle and bustle, I saw my cup as half-full. I had talented children, a helpful husband, and a refreshing place to sit in the shade—many things for which to give thanks.

We can have this asset—thankfulness—in our lives all of the time, but only if we're willing to work for it. Like many people, I am often tempted to see the cup as half-empty. But when I do that, I lose sight of all I have to be thankful for. I lose my contentment.

Have you ever reflected upon how closely thankfulness and contentment stand? I think they walk hand in hand.

When my children were very small and it was sometimes a challenge to talk and reason with them, I always made sure to hide the Christmas catalog when it arrived in the mail each fall. Letting them look at it certainly would have occupied them for hours, but it simply wouldn't be worth the disappointment it often brought. As wide eyes scanned those pages, taking in the shiny new toys and games, their bikes in the garage, their games on the shelves, and their clothes in the closet no longer seemed good enough. The reality of the well-worn and familiar pales in comparison to the sparkling and brand-new.

Like I did for my children, I find that I must still take away the Christmas catalogs in my own life. For instance, I do not subscribe to the popular house and garden magazines you find on the market today, for they seem to have the same effect on me that the Christmas catalog had on my children. My lovely home and great yard lose their attractiveness when placed beside the glossy pages of America's finest homes, and suddenly I feel as if I do not have enough. I lose my contentment, and thankfulness slips away from me.

Please don't see this as a negative statement about American advertising, although it would be easy to fall into that. Instead, please see it as a gentle reminder concerning daily contentment and thankfulness. For magazines do not show us pictures of bushes that have seen better days, days *before* the basketball has bounced into their branches dozens of times. Nor do the magazine covers ever sport homes where the vinyl siding is showing signs of wear and tear. Yet what about the families who delight in shooting baskets together, then gathering in the cozy house with a plateful of cookies and mugs of hot cocoa to share love and laughter? Now *that* is a great story to feature on the pages of our lives.

Today's media thinks they are selling us the loveliest picture of all, a picture that sets the standard for true contentment. If we're to fit into this picture, we must drive cars that sell for a year's wages, and we must own homes that contain the most up-to-date appliances, carpeting, furniture, and accessories. But is that really the way to true contentment?

A favorite verse from the fourth chapter of Philippians comes to mind at this point, the one that speaks about being content in every situation: "I am not saying this because I am in need, for I have learned to be content whatever the circumstances" (Philippians 4:11 NIV). It would be infinitely easier for us to obey that verse if we made thankfulness a daily practice in our homes.

By the way, the bushes in front of my house have seen better days, and unless the siding gets washed every year, it becomes very dusty. The outside of our house has had contact with

> *Yet what about the families who delight in shooting baskets together, then gathering in the cozy house with a plateful of cookies and mugs of hot cocoa to share love and laughter? Now that is a great story to feature on the pages of our lives.*

everything from the foursquare ball to the lawn tractor, but we love our home. It's full of warmth and memories. It's cool in the summer and warm in winter. The carpet in the living room and hall had to be replaced recently, and it's time to repaint in some of the rooms, but even if those jobs are not accomplished for years, I have a multitude of things for which I can be thankful. After all, I've chosen to be thankful for the things that matter most.

My cottage is clean and weatherproof;

my furniture sufficient and commodious.

All I see has made me thankful.

CHARLOTTE BRONTË

Family

I love my family.

I grew up with just one brother, but my cousins—
three boys and a girl—grew up in the house behind ours.
Our backyards joined, and when I think of the adventures we
had together, my face bursts into a big smile—we're talking fun!
There was no end to the games and activities we could think up
to play. We built forts in trees and constructed vehicles from old
plywood and rusty nails. Have you ever tried to straighten a nail
with a rock so you could pound it into a two-by-four?

To say the least, the summers were nonstop.

One summer in particular stands out—the summer we got the ducks. Our great-grandmother was still living but she was not able to get out. So we decided to bring the summertime indoors to her. My cousins came up with the fantastic plan to load the ducks into a gunnysack and bring them into her bedroom. My brother and I wished we had thought of the idea first, but we good-naturedly went along with our cousins. The little ducks were still fairly small and fuzzy, but one outgoing duckling had already developed an outrageously loud quack. This little white duck "talked" the whole time we were in the room. I'm not sure if my great-grandmother enjoyed it as much as we did, but we certainly meant well. My memories of those carefree summers, full of family and fun, are very sweet.

Now the generations have shifted.

Today my three children are part of a throng of fourteen cousins, whose varied ages span almost a nineteen-year period. They look forward to family gatherings with great anticipation, for they love to laugh and play together whenever everyone unites. I am always so pleased to see how the older cousins take the younger ones on outings and make sure they feel special and included.

A third-grade ritual at my children's school has been to share with their classmates about their family. As each child entered the third grade, he or she looked forward to taking part in this special show-and-tell. Our family has had such fun selecting photographs that showed the kids in their younger years. I grin in delight when I see where we've been, and my heart fills with excitement when I think about where we're headed. Unlike some mothers, I never wish for my children to be babies again. I'm enjoying our present life too much.

I must admit, though, that I don't always look forward to the start of school each fall, for it interrupts our summertime fun. But for my kids' sake as well as my own, we use this time to have a positive outlook and talk about things for which we are thankful. We're grateful for the chance to see old friends and meet new ones, the routine of classes and school activities, the snow that will soon fall, and even the opportunity to learn and study. All of these are things for which to give thanks, even though we may not always realize it. For instance, it's too easy to see learning as simply a chore. I know that it's work—often hard work—but how thankful we can be for our minds! They're really quite amazing. And when they are used to think well, they're spectacular.

School sports are another big area of thankfulness for me. As of this writing, none of my children drive. I am Mom's Taxi Service when it comes to practice and occasional out-of-town events. The kids need my enthusiasm during these times. When practice starts to become ho-hum or when the team has lost every game of the season, the reasons to get up and try again have to be bigger than the thrill of winning. This is when we can be thankful for healthy bodies and the ability to play the games we love. Certainly the driving and sched-uling take effort on my part, but they are things I'm willing to do when I see the happiness in my children's eyes when they are complimented after a good practice or score the game-winning shot.

I feel the same way about my household chores. Thankfulness is my choice here. I can iron my husband's shirts, grateful for the marriage we share, or I can do it in bitterness that only serves to upset the whole family. It's very helpful that Bob is thankful for the work I do, but even if no one notices my efforts, I can be proud that I did a fine job.

Will my children

realize what a

precious gift

thankfulness is?

I love the family I might have in the future, and already I'm grateful for them.

I'll admit that it might be a bit premature for me to think of grandchildren while my own kids are still in school, but I can't help but imagine the fun we'll have. When I visit my grandchildren someday, I hope that I'll be greeted by children delighted to see me instead of by kids who are only happy if I've brought them something. Like most parents, I sometimes worry. Will my children realize what a precious gift thankfulness is? Will they pass it on to their own children? I hope and pray they do. So far they've given me great reason to believe that they will.

Not long ago our daughter stumbled as she walked across the carpet. She began to complain and then caught herself. She looked up and told me she needed to be thankful that she had feet. I smiled at her. In that instant my daughter understood that thankfulness is a choice, and I was proud that she wisely made the best choice.

The supreme happiness in life is the conviction that we are loved.

VICTOR HUGO

The Little Things

Are you ever thankful for tissues or electric lights?

Do you take your dishwasher or washing machine for granted?

Does your car start most days and get you to where you need to be?

Are you thankful to have a refrigerator and freezer that

keep your food fresh and cold? And are you grateful

for your garbage collector?

Years ago I heard Rich DeVos, president of an international

company, tell a story about how he went out to see the garbage

man one day in order to thank him. The audience laughed

hysterically when Mr. DeVos recounted that the perplexed garbage

man asked him if he was going out or just getting home.

I laughed, too. But then Mr. DeVos asked us if we were thankful for our garbage man. "Just let him miss your house for a few weeks, then you'll be pretty glad to see him," he quipped. We all laughed, but we all understood his point.

Now that I think about it, I realize that I have a tendency to take many things in my life for granted. Running water. Electricity. Paved streets. Indoor plumbing. Carpeted floors. It's so easy to do, and when it happens the result is not a pretty sight. I become discontented and a frown crowds out my smile.

Now, I don't wish for you to see me as a woman who walks around her house and yard in a state of euphoria over everything she sees. But I do think my heart works best when it beats strong with thankfulness for all that has been given to me—the blessings I enjoy every day. Not everyone can take delight in a car that runs well, but having a car—just about any car— is truly a blessing. And I can't say that cold air never sneaks in through my window frames, but I'm far from homeless. I'm richly blessed.

We have some lovely large trees in our front yard. Come fall, they drop leaves in great piles, leaves that make their way all across the flowerbeds in the front yard, up onto the porch, and even into the house on the soles of our shoes. Some years we're better at keeping up with the raking than other years. And it's easy to become frustrated when you work hard raking one day only to find a fresh carpet of leaves adorning the lawn the next morning. I can let this affect me; I can lose my thankfulness.

Or I can be grateful for majestic trees that give us shade in the summer and for autumn leaves of the most beautiful hues imaginable. I can even give praise for children who are strong and willing to work when those leaves fall.

We had some wind here recently. And not just any wind, but the sixty-mile-per-hour variety. I've heard that some of the windows in Russian buildings have quadruple-paned glass. I think we could have used those in this recent storm! We have double-paned windows, but they weren't much help during that day of strong winds. The furnace kicked on more frequently, and we all bundled up a bit more.

The wind saw to it that the last of the leaves left town, or at least exited our yard. The cracks in the siding will have to wait to be fixed until warmer weather sets in, but the double-paned windows will keep out the icy air and we're glad our water and heat work fine. Yes, we will be ready to meet the frosty days and nights.

We won't need to head to the outhouse in the backyard or carry water from the well. Not that those things would be the end of the world, but we *can* be thankful for the conveniences that make our lives a little bit easier. We can shut fast the windows and doors, knowing we'll be warm in our home and also in our hearts as we count up the many little things with which we are blessed.

On second thought, maybe the word "little" isn't the one I want to use at all.

Blessings

I am beginning to learn that it is the sweet, simple things of life which are the real ones after all.

LAURA INGALLS WILDER

Girlfriends

I celebrated a birthday not long ago. It was a landmark occasion because I went from being thirty-something to the big four-oh! One of the cards I received had a picture of two older ladies on the front. Probably sixty-something, they both had hairnets covering their white curls. They also wore slippers and their dresses were of the not-so-fashionable housedress style. In the photo they are dancing. The front of the card says, *If we have to grow old...* And the inside message reads, *I'll let you lead.* This was very funny to me because Jackie, who sent me the birthday greeting, is six years older than I am.

Right now I don't feel like I can find adequate words to describe how thankful I am for friends, but I must try. Over the years friends have been lifesavers for me.

I adore my husband, but when the Bible talks about female relationships, I know that God understands how much women need each other. I never leave Bob out of things, but my girlfriends are the people who know how the heart of a mother feels when my son leaves on his first out-of-town basketball game.

Two ladies of the Bible who give me a wonderful example of the friendships between women are Mary and Elizabeth. The first chapter of Luke tells us that when Mary was expecting Christ, she paid a visit to Elizabeth. I love how the two friends talk about God here. Read the first few verses from the Magnificat to see what I mean: "And Mary said: 'My soul exalts the Lord, and my spirit has rejoiced in God my Savior....For the Mighty One has done great things for me; and holy is His name'" (Luke 1:46-49 NASB).

I'm challenged by the example of Mary and Elizabeth to ask myself what I talk about with my friends. It's so desperately important that our closest friendships be built around Jesus Christ.

I have known unconditional love from so many dear women. I'll never forget the time I first met my husband's family. I went home with him for Thanksgiving before we were married. We spent a great weekend with his family, and on Sunday, as Bob and I prepared to head back to school in Michigan, his sister Jane stopped me and told me how wonderful it was that I had been able to come. She said that even though Bob had written that I looked like Jane and acted like Ann, that I wasn't either of them. I'll never forget how she said it: "You're not Jane and you're not Ann. You're Lori, and it's Lori we love."

She offered me unconditional love and friendship at that very important moment. Four years after Bob and I were married and moved to Wisconsin from California, my sister-in-law continued to offer her friendship. Jane took a map of the Madison area and highlighted her house, showing how to get there from our small town. She also marked places that I might like to visit. Our friendship has done nothing but grow ever since.

I am doubly and triply blessed that my mother and mother-in-law are also some of my closest friends. These older believers in my life mean so much to me. I can't say that I never grow impatient with them or wish they would sometimes do things my way, but their gentle behavior and loving kindness speak volumes as to the work God has done in their lives.

I can say honestly that I want to be like Pearl, my mother, and Helen, my mother-in-law, "sweeter as the years go by." I want to have their wisdom and quiet understanding. Even at their ages, when some might think they should have everything all figured out, they still share with me the things with which they struggle. And this encourages me. Times of questioning and dealing with problems are not what I would wish for these two ladies, but it's also comforting to know that God is going to keep refining me and sticking with me even when I'm well past the big four-oh.

Donny Finley

Doors

I cannot think of another artist who paints doors
in the magnificent way that Donny Finley does. I can gaze
at his enchanting paintings for hours and, because
I'm blessed with an active imagination, I can think up
all kinds of scenarios about what's going on inside.

I see his painting *Inner Light* as the home
of a gentle grandmotherly woman, round and graying
with age. Her smile is boundless when the children
from the village knock on her door, knowing she always will
welcome them in with a plate of cookies fresh from the oven.

Cottage Roses is the home of a younger woman, her twin girls not
yet school age. Midafternoon will find the little girls at the front
door. They peer through its windows, watching for their two older
brothers to arrive home with books and slates in hand.

They repeat this ritual of anticipation, all four children now, when it's time for Father to return from work. Mother doesn't mind. It allows her a few quiet moments to make last-minute preparations for supper.

Climbing Roses is still a mystery to me. I haven't quite decided who inhabits the house, but I can almost feel the sunshine falling on that doorway and see my own footsteps meandering down the path. Perhaps this painting includes me, and I'm on my way to the home of a good friend who has invited me for coffee.

I love being a fiction writer and giving way to my imagination, but even more than that, I love the doors in my life that do not require any imagination at all, just remembering.

I was privileged to enter one of the favorite doors in my life time and time again. I loved Grandma's door. We never knew what to expect when we went over to her house, for her door was often painted a new color. She would go on painting sprees, and the trim, steps, doors, and even planters would emerge in a bright new shade. But one thing never changed—all of us grandkids were always welcome in her home, any time of the day or night. Grandma lived right next door to my family, which had its good points as well as its not-so-good points. We felt like we had another mother. When we were trying to get away with things, we resented another pair of eyes upon our actions. When we were hurt and needed comfort, Grandma's presence was a soothing balm to our skinned knees or wounded feelings. Looking back, I'm thankful for her nearness and for the love she showed us. I'm so thankful to have had her for so long, as she lived to be 94 years old. I smile now when I think of her, standing at her freshly painted door.

The entryway to my in-laws' back door was swathed in shadows when I arrived at their home in 1979. They weren't my in-laws then, but I was in love with their son. Bob had let me know ahead of time how they would greet me. *Dad will shake your hand and Mom will give you a big hug.* I was delighted when it happened just that way. We met in the back hallway just inside that door, and they greeted me for the first time. Their instant love and acceptance of me has been a source of great peace and joy for many years.

The dark green door in the first home my husband and I bought was rather thin and shabby. If we'd lived in the Midwest in those days, we would have frozen. Nevertheless, this was our home—our *first* home—and we were proud of it. I had heard all my life about the writer Jack London, and now we were living on a street that was named after him. And wouldn't you know it, three families from our church lived right in the neighborhood. We lived in that house for only a few years, but our loving neighbors taught us so much and sent us off to our next destination with such love and caring that their kind faces and encouraging words still linger sweetly in my mind.

Yet another blessed door in my memory offers an inside look. It's the door of my hospital room, and it has been shut as the nurse has thoughtfully left me alone with my brand-new baby boy. Gazing at him, I realized what my own mother had felt many years ago when she held me in her arms. I looked into his precious little face and even then knew that he would have to become a parent himself to truly understand the emotions I was feeling.

I still look into my son's face, and those of his siblings, and know that they can't quite understand what goes on inside my heart. I don't have to tell them. I just need to imagine the front door to my own home and let them know that for my precious children, the door is always open.

Still round the corner there may wait, a new road or a secret gate.

J.R.R. Tolkein

Persistence

One spring persistence came into my life in the form
of two house finches and two robins.

I'm not known for my green thumb. Just remembering to water
plants is a chore for me. So about three years ago I came up
with the brilliant idea of hanging silk ivy plants in baskets on
the porch. They looked wonderful. Even up close the ivy
looked like the real thing, and the hanging wire baskets
matched our shutters to perfection.

It didn't take long for me to see that the birds
thought the baskets of ivy were perfect, too.

The first season I tried going out and shooing the birds away every time they tried to nest. Sometimes they managed to get a stick or a small branch into the pot, but I was diligent about keeping them away—for about a week, whereupon I gave up, took the baskets down, and put them in the garage.

That's right. The birds were persistent. I gave up.

The next year I tried again. Come spring, I hung the pots, positioned the ivy just right, and stood back with pleasure to view the lovely display. But the birds were quick this time. It only took them about an hour to spot the ivy, and because the baskets sit right outside my office window, I found myself getting up and down numerous times to try to persuade them to build their nests elsewhere, but to no avail. As I had done the previous year, I gave up under their tenacity and took the baskets into the garage.

The third year was different. Not for the birds, mind you. They were as persistent as ever. I, however, gave up in a different way. I didn't move the baskets. Sure enough, within a matter of days we had Mr. and Mrs. Robin at home in one basket and Mr. and Mrs. Finch setting up residence in the other, busily making nests and happy as clams at high tide.

At first I was delighted. At first I thought, "I shouldn't have been fighting this. This is great! We'll be able to see baby birds in flight."

That was before Mrs. Robin laid more eggs than the nest could handle, and one of the eggs spilled out too early on the unforgiving concrete of the front porch. My delight also turned to disappointment when I realized that while Mr. and Mrs. Finch were very meticulous about their own home—the nest—they couldn't care less about the mess they made of mine. The house wall and porch were filthy—a not-so-minor distraction from the cheery pots of ivy and the cute little birds.

But those bird families did teach me something—persistence. They wanted to nest on that front porch. I mean, they wanted it badly. Their persistence got to me, and I gave in.

Their steadfast natures reminded me of myself when I determined to write my first book. I was the mother of two very little boys that year, one a toddler and the other just two years older. I still played with them, I still loved them and made sure they were taken care of, but every spare moment I had, I wrote.

I remember the television was in Bob's and my bedroom. I would sprawl across the bed, pen and paper laid out in front of me, and write. The boys would already be in the room watching their afternoon cartoons. As soon as I joined them, they would come and sit on my back. I can still picture the scene of the three of us relaxed together on the bed. At times they would have me watch something with them, or I would look up when I heard their little giggles, but for the most part, I was persistent. I wanted to write that book. And write that book I did.

Did I perplex people who couldn't quite comprehend my determination? I must have, but I'm thankful for the times in my life when I've been persistent. Many times I tend to give up all too easily.

It's a challenge when God is that persistent with me. I can't believe how many times His Word tells me to love others and pray for them. It's so easy to love some people and not others,

I love the gospels. I love looking at the way Jesus Christ worked with the disciples—His authority and patience guiding everything He taught and did.

but God does not give us that option. How many times have I been unlovable, but His love for me was as persistent and constant as God is Himself? I must do the same for those around me.

I love the gospels. I love looking at the way Jesus Christ worked with the disciples—His authority and patience guiding everything He taught and did. I can sit down to read a complete copy of God's Word, but the disciples had to try and learn through parables told by the Man Himself. Sometimes I envy them their experience; most often I don't. Like me, they didn't understand things the first time they heard them. Like me, they often thought of themselves instead of the great work that was being placed on their shoulders.

But Jesus Christ persisted. He taught them, loved them, and worked with them until it was time for Him to leave, and they continued the work He had started.

And that's what I am—a work that's been started. Jesus Christ persisted with me, too. Through His Word, He tells me He's never going to give up (Hebrews 13:5). He assures me there is no sin that He's not willing to forgive (1 John 1:9). And as for worries, His shoulders are the broadest and most able to bear every one of the anxieties that persist in hounding me (1 Peter 5:7).

God's persistence shouts to us from His Word and consistently in His creation as well. He even made the little birds that would not give up until they had built their nests on my front porch. I'm not sure I'll hang the baskets of ivy outside next spring, but I'm still thankful for those birds and the way they made me think and remember to be thankful for the gift of persistence.

. . .and let us run with patience

Persistence

the race that is set before us.

HEBREWS 12:1

Give thanks unto the Lord, for he is good, his mercy endureth forever.

PSALM 106:1

Christmas

Whenever I fly into the San Francisco airport and head north
to visit my family, I always pass by a certain shopping center.
It's not a huge place, but it has a restaurant I like, and at one time
it had a Christmas store that fascinated me.

The first time I discovered this store, we were running
short on time and I didn't get a chance to really look in it.
But I remember being charmed by the idea of a store
that carried Christmas things all year long.

The second time I came across a store like this was at Pier 39
in San Francisco. I had plenty of time on my hands then,
and with a sense of wonder I walked through the shop.

Many Christmas trees were displayed, each beautifully decorated with every imaginable type of ornament. You could buy fat shiny bulbs or tiny wooden trains, shimmering tinsel, colorful lights, delicate glass angels, cozy knit stockings, and even a variety of wreaths to be displayed year after year. The store was so bright and festive, you couldn't help but smile. My sons were fairly small at that time and I remember one of them trying to carry on a conversation with an enormous stuffed Santa Claus that sat near the entrance. He thought it was a real man!

I also remember thinking, "I wish it were Christmas right now."

As I remember my experience in that enchanting store, I wonder why it has to be cold outside before I can get into the spirit of things. Or why, as the holiday season grows near, I've been known to tell Bob, "We've got to get a tree; it doesn't feel like Christmas without a tree."

Being a lover of words, I decided to go to my dictionary to see if Webster could shed any light on this holiday. And this is what I found: *A Christian feast on December 25th that commemorates the birth of Christ and is usually observed as a legal holiday.*

Now I know that the dictionary meant *feast* in the usual sense of the word—food and fellowship enjoyed around the table. But as I began to picture what a feast Christ should be to us all year long, my heart dwelt on the word in another way.

Why must I wait until the lights are strung and a few cards have arrived before I begin to celebrate *my* feast? I admit that it's rather hard to think of Christmas when you're washing swimsuits and towels for another day of cooling off at the pool, and in order to make the temperature comfortable, the air conditioner has to be running at all times. But if there is a feast to be found lying within the manger bed, shouldn't I hunger after that feast no matter what the season, rain or shine, snow or heat?

Matthew 1:23 says, "Behold, the virgin shall be with child, and shall bear a Son, and they shall call His name Immanuel, which translated means, 'God with us'" (NASB).

I'm thankful that God is with us—not just in December—but all year through.

CHRISTMAS IN JULY

Is it possible to think of Christmas when shopping for swimming gear?
Can we really picture the Christ Child, as summer vacation draws near?

After all, there's no snow upon the ground or crisp cold feeling in the air.
And isn't summer the very time we're to throw off all our care?

There are no trees with tinsel or stockings hung with joy.
Can we really concentrate on Yule tidings when the stores aren't stuffed with toys?

And will we really be less busy when December rolls around?
Will hearts turn automatically to the place where Christ is found?

Maybe it's a heart condition, making the weather a flimsy reason.
Can our hearts overflow with Christmas joy no matter what the season?

May our hearts be ever challenged even as the sun beats on the ground,
To look to the nativity where all hope can surely be found.

37

Guys

I'm thankful for the men in my life. I know some great guys. I'd like to tell you about a few.

Andy built my mother's screen porch one fall. He did the job on his own, even though he has several men who work for him. Andy is one of those guys who is completely honest and real. When he hurts, he cries. If he's upset, he'll tell you. But most often it's his joy in the Lord that is contagious.

I went down to visit my mom one day when Andy was working on the porch. I was surprised to find him alone.

"Andy, you're on your own!"

"You bet. Just me and the Trinity!"

I like that. I like it a lot.

Todd is another guy in my life. He's my neighbor from down the street. He writes beautifully. I love his Christmas cards, and his poetry, and especially his way with people. I don't know if Todd has to work hard to be compassionate, but he does such a great job at it that I imagine it comes naturally. Todd is more than just a neighbor; he's also one of our pastors. He never brings us sermons that he hasn't already worked on, worked through, and learned himself. For instance, he spoke on parenting for several weeks. He challenged us to have straight "arrows" in our quiver. And he spoke from his own heart about his own experiences.

One of my favorite stories he told involves two of his four sons. Todd came home one night to find these two sons in a complaining sort of mood. While still teaching the boys an important lesson, he playfully rushed them around the kitchen and exclaimed with wonder as he showed them all the food in the cupboards. Next he took them to their rooms and, in a voice filled with excitement, pointed out to them the warm beds they could sleep in that night. I think they even went to the closet and had a party over all the clothes they had to wear!

As Todd told us this we laughed, but we still took seriously the importance of the message. I think his sons did, too.

Phil is our other great pastor. Like Todd, he never says, "Do as I say, not as I do." He puts himself through the paces of God's Word and then teaches us what he's discovered.

I'm thankful that Phil isn't just spouting his own ideas, but instead giving us God's. Although I love his preaching, I don't always want to hear what he says from the pulpit; sometimes it hurts too much. It's so easy to want to change other people and not myself. Yet God says it doesn't work that way. I'm so thankful that Phil is working on himself first and then sharing with me so that I can adjust the person I see in the mirror.

Bob, of course, is the love of my life. I can't say that about any other man. Just Bob. I might not show him that every day because I'm not always easy to live with. But I am secure in the love we share. I'm thankful that he never gives up on me and continues to love me.

Bob is not a quitter. He never has been. His father has always liked to compete, too. He was not one of those guys who would race his kids and go easy on them. Bob would just run all the harder to beat him.

A lack of thankfulness can make me want to quit. I wasn't always thankful for my husband. He tried to be the leader in our home and I didn't want that, but if he's going to follow the Bible's commands, he has no choice. If he's going to stand before God and answer for the job he's done, he needs to read the job description and then do his best to follow it.

In a time when "girl power" is strongly promoted and many women simply do not want anyone telling them what to do—most especially a man—I'm thankful for the men in my life. I'm thankful that they lead by example.

I'm also thankful that the men in my life …do not attempt to lord over me and treat me like a servant. My heart needs to be that of a servant, and this is something that is often surprisingly easy to do when I know I am loved.

I'm thankful for the guys in my life, thankful that I am ready to let them be who God wants them to be, so I can be the woman God intended.

When I was determined to lead, it was chaos. It took a humbling inside of me to admit that God had a better plan. It took a humbling inside of me to see that I didn't have all the answers and that the ideas of others were actually much better than my own. I fought this for years, but nothing compares with the joy and peace I now have knowing I don't need to be in control of every situation.

I'm also thankful that the men in my life, most especially Bob, do not attempt to lord over me and treat me like a servant. My heart needs to be that of a servant, and this is something that is often surprisingly easy to do when I know I am loved.

When my children play on basketball or soccer teams, it's easy for them to mistake the coach's instructions as unfair criticism of them as individuals. It's a great temptation for them to quit and go off alone to feel sorry for themselves. But they need to keep on improving, keep on trying a little harder. I need to do the same thing in my relationships. I can see my pastors' or Bob's rebukes and instruction as them criticizing me, or I can see them as acts of love. I choose to believe I am cherished and that they want the best for me.

Do I sound like I'm living in the dark ages? Interestingly enough, I've lived my life both ways, and when you've experienced both worlds, you're blessed with a front-row seat on the action. I've decided where I want to be based on years of experience. I'm thankful for the guys in my life, thankful that I am ready to let them be who God wants them to be, so I can be the woman God intended.

Right now it would be easy to see me as the most *un*liberated woman on the face of the earth. I'm happy to tell you that I'm as unfettered as I have ever been.

I would maintain that thanks are the highest form of thought,

and that gratitude is happiness doubled by wonder.

G.K. CHESTERTON

Church Cleaning

A number of years back, when it was my turn to clean
the church, I asked God for a blessing and He gave me one.
The task was not one I was dreading, but neither
was I jumping for joy. Yet on this particular day I was pleased
to learn that I would have the privilege of cleaning the church
with my mother-in-law, a delightful lady and treasured friend.

You'll never guess what my mother-in-law loves to do.
She loves to clean bathrooms! She scrubs and polishes
and cleans bathrooms, even going so far as to get down
on her hands and knees to wash the floor.

She also loves to take care of dirty toddlers at bath time. It wasn't long ago that I could have provided one for her on a daily basis. She loves taking a grimy child to the tub and then returning with a clean, towel-wrapped little person, ready to be dressed and cuddled.

Her finding pleasure in such small things is a good example to me. It's no wonder that the two of us can't be together and not have fun.

Once we arrived at the church, I think we split up for some of the time. Mom went down to the basement and I started toward the foyer and sanctuary. And although the time spent with my beloved cleaning companion was certainly delightful, I was most blessed when I was alone cleaning the railing that sits in front of the pulpit, and then dusting the podium itself.

I cleaned the pulpit and then stood behind it for a moment to look out over the empty pews. It's not a view I see often. I took new notice of the symmetry of those pews—the way the aisles angled down to the front, and took note of the rich color of the oak woodwork along with the nice blend of the carpet. The orderliness of it made me think of God, and I could have stood there a long time but I had work to do. Before I returned to my cleaning, however, words came to mind from a song sung by Steve Green. In "The Mission" he says:

To love the Lord our God

Is the heartbeat of the mission

The spring from which our service overflows

Across the street

Or around the world

The mission's still the same

Proclaim and live the Truth

In Jesus' name!

I'm thankful to be a part of the Black Earth Congregational Church, where we are the "across-the-street" mission. Sundays see those pews filled with people from every walk of life—the saved and unsaved, the hurting and joyful, the searchers and those who know why they are there. The list is more than I can name.

But on that day it was just a privilege for me to clean when it was my turn and to play a small part in reaching out to those who would sit in the pews and worship with me in the House of God. I was thankful that I could do my small part in His amazing plan.

Dad

Empty chairs or benches that sit surrounded by flowers
in a garden remind me of my father. I'm not sure why,
because he was never a prolific gardener or even one to just
sit outdoors, but there's something serene and a little bit
lonely about flowers surrounding an empty bench.
Maybe that's why this scene makes me think of him.

My dad passed away in the summer of 1995.
Some days his death feels very recent and some days
it seems like it's been forever. Perhaps you can never prepare
for the moment, but we were unaware that he would leave us
so soon. He hadn't been enjoying the best of health, but we all
thought he was doing fairly well. So it was rather numbing
when we received the phone call telling us he was gone.

We went to be with my mother immediately. Having booked the flight so late, our family was spread out all over the plane, but for the first part of the journey I was able to sit beside my daughter. I felt like my heart might break, but as I looked down at her almost-six-year-old form, I was thankful that at her age I still had my dad.

Dad hadn't planned to go anywhere the day he died. This was obvious by the way we found things. His Bible was placed under his pajamas, which were sitting where he always left them. His daily ritual was to read his Bible each morning and then get dressed. A few ads and magazines sat by his chair, waiting to be read. But even though it looked like he hadn't made any travel plans, I knew that deep down he was ready to leave this earth. Deep down he had made the step of faith that only counts if it's made in Jesus Christ, the step that ensures a heavenly home for all of eternity. I was sad that I wouldn't have my dad here on earth to hug and laugh with again, but I was comforted to know that he was at peace and rest in an amazing place. Not because of anything he did, but because he trusted in Christ's work on the cross.

I've trusted, too. I think I'm able to be thankful more often because of that trust.

Not all of us are spared what I was spared by having my father pass away more than halfway across the country. I did not have to hear an ambulance siren, watch paramedics work to save my father's life, or sit in a hospital waiting room, anxious for news of his condition. My final memory of my dad is a good one. I last saw him at the fortieth wedding anniversary celebration we'd had for him and my mom early that year. We had spent ten days together, laughing and talking and rejoicing in a marriage that had lasted forty years and held a promise of many more to come. Dad was gone four months later. I wish I had been there at the time for my mom, but I can be grateful for how she was strong before, during, and after our arrival.

I ache for the way some people have to say goodbye, but that was not the way God had it planned for me. I can still feel my father's hug and the way he would stroke my cheek with the backs of his fingers, his eyes smiling into mine. I can recall what his voice sounded like as we spoke on the phone just hours before his death. He's gone from my life for awhile, but I can still see rainbows amid the clouds. I can still choose to be thankful.

However great our difficulties or deep even our sorrows, there is room for thankfulness....As someone has said, there are here three precious ideas: "careful for nothing; prayerful for everything; and thankful for anything." We always get more by being thankful for what God has done for us.

D.L. MOODY

Thorns

My daughter threw her arms around me last week and said,
"I just love you, Mom." I'll be the first to admit that such a gesture does a
lot for a mother's heart. It's not quite so uplifting, however,
to see that her lunch box still remains where she dropped it
and the socks I thought she'd put in the wash are instead
dangling out of the tops of her tennis shoes.

Where is my thankfulness during those times?

For many years, my phone has rung on one special day.
It was always my father on the other end wishing me a happy anniversary.
I, in turn, delightedly wished him a happy birthday.
My husband and I were married on Dad's forty-eighth birthday.
Over the years we shared that day time and again. But that will not
stop the phone from ringing even when the news isn't good.

Such news came a few weeks after Dad's sixty-third birthday. My
mother's voice is in shock as she tells me he's gone.

Where is my thankfulness during those times?

My path, like everyone else's, is not always bordered by roses. This is something most of us know only too well. When the flowers are blooming and the sun is shining, thankfulness is swift on our lips. A quick smile is present and laughter is never far away. Loved ones are healthy. The kids' grades are up. Even the dandelions on the lawn seem cheery. In those times, it's very easy to forget the pain of the past or to be insensitive to a friend who is hurting.

Could there be a way to store thankfulness for the moments when we most need it? Maybe that sounds impossible, but I believe I can draw upon stored peace and thankfulness when I find myself hurting and remember that even amid the pain, I have something for which to be appreciative. In my own life, remembering that God is sovereign—absolutely in control at all times—is paramount. If I thought I was just wandering around here on my own, I would have every reason to feel lost and desperate. But I don't. I know the reason I am here, and I know the One who placed me in this life, in these circumstances.

Maybe it's difficult for you to hear this. Perhaps you're one of those people who does not believe that God can be all-powerful and good at the same time, but I caution you on this. Do not put God in a box. Do not place God in such a way in your life that you only want Him out when *you* feel you need Him. You need Him always.

We like to ask ourselves many questions concerning God and His place in our lives. Where is He when we see television programs that show the plight of starving children? We long for God to step out in a powerful way and change things, but please God, don't tap me on the shoulder when I'm cheating on my taxes. After all, the government has so much, so what if I turned in some receipts that weren't really business expenses?

And where is God when drunken driving laws are lenient and a third-time offender runs a child down in the street? What kind of good God allows that? But God, don't knock on my car door when my boyfriend and I have found a secluded place to be alone. I mean, we're going to get married. Why wait?

God in a box. We like the idea of keeping Him handy and ready to pull out whenever something is bothering us, so He can fix it and make us feel better. But stay in the box, God, if I'm comfortable doing what I'm doing or believe it's right.

As you can see, it's very easy for us to accuse God of not being on the job. Yet, Scripture is very clear about God's power, sovereignty, wisdom, and ability to intervene. I sometimes wonder, painful as the news is to watch, what might have happened if God wasn't directing behind the scenes. It's something I may never know. Airplanes go down, hundreds die, and we ask what could be worse?

I'll tell you.

A people, a nation, a world, that is completely apathetic to God. Indifference is a much scarier place to be than on a crashing airplane, but not many people want to think this way.

Hold everything, you say. I didn't bargain for this, Lori. I thought this book would help me to be thankful. Right now I'm growing more and more depressed.

Dear friend, I would not be honest with you if I didn't explain the process I follow. No matter how sad the news reports are, I can find peace and thankfulness because my faith rests in Someone larger than my own abilities, Someone more powerful than anything I will ever encounter on this earth. Without that faith, this world would be a very hopeless, unthankful place to be. But I rejoice that my faith carries me to another place.

The news will continue to broadcast stories that are difficult to watch. People I love and care for will continue to know pain, as will I from time to time, but I can still rest in hope and thankfulness. I'm not laughing with glee all the time or sporting a permanent grin to present to the world, but deep in my heart I know that God would never allow anything into my life that I could not handle. His Word promises that very thing. I don't know about you, but I can't think of anything for which to be more thankful.

In the deepest night of trouble and sorrow God gives us so much to be thankful for that we need never cease our singing. With all our wisdom and foresight we can take a lesson in gladness and gratitude from the happy bird that sings all night, as if the day were not enough to tell its joy.

SAMUEL TAYLOR COLERIDGE

Living Water

When Bob and I were still living in Santa Rosa,
I used to rise early, long before Bob was ready for work,
and go to one of our spare bedrooms for my quiet time.
I would sit at the big desk in that room, in front of the window—
drapes open—and look out at the hills that rose up
beyond our backyard.

One morning I noticed for the first time a cross carved
into the side of one of those hills. I couldn't believe I'd never
seen it before. I watched as the days went by, the grass
grew greener, and the cross became more and more clear.

I began to think of it as my cross. When I prayed I would look right at it, and sometimes I would cry with thanksgiving for what that cross represented—God's saving grace.

Winters in Santa Rosa mean rain, lots of it. As we got deeper and deeper into the months of the rainy season, each day I enjoyed that cross, so clear against the vivid green of the mountain.

Summers in Santa Rosa are dry, incredibly so. And as spring came and summer approached, things began to take on their familiar parched look, and I noticed a change on the mountainside. By early summer every blade of grass was dried up and brown, and the cross on the hillside became almost invisible.

I thought how like my own life that cross was. When I stay near the fountain of living water, my Bible, reading it every day—staying fresh and green—then the cross is evident in my life to all who care to look.

But when I choose to wander away from the fountain, I grow parched and faint. When the world looks at me during those times, they see nothing different in me, nothing special, nothing to encourage them to ask about the hope they see in my countenance.

Later when we still lived in that same house, I became pregnant with our first child. My friends and family knew not to call me in the afternoons because that was when I would be taking a nap. I was not able to pamper myself with any of my other pregnancies, so I'm glad I did with the first one.

I recall having cravings of different kinds during those nine months, and one of them was for watermelon. I remember waking up from those naps and the house being very hot.

And because I was quite pregnant and had been asleep for several hours, the first place I needed to visit was the bathroom. I would be warm and thirsty, and I remember so clearly that as I would finish up in that small room and wash my hands, I would deliberately not take a drink of cold water, not even so much as a little taste.

My hands would be cool and still a little damp as I then headed out to the kitchen and took the crisp watermelon from the refrigerator. My first bite would be right from the center, no seeds, juicy and ice-cold.

There is no way to describe such gratification, such satisfying refreshment. The only thing that ever matches it for me—in fact, far surpasses it—is when my spirit is dry and I go to God with my deep thirst. I believe with all my heart that He is the Living Water, and in Him my thirst is quenched and I am ever satisfied.

John 4:13-14 says, "Jesus answered and said to her, 'Everyone who drinks of this water shall thirst again; but whoever drinks of the water that I shall give him shall never thirst; but the water that I shall give him shall become in him a well of water springing up to eternal life'" (NASB).

I am so thankful that He is my source of life eternal.

I began to think of it as my cross. When I prayed I would look right at it, and sometimes I would cry with thanksgiving for what that cross represented— God's saving grace.

Honesty

I must tell you the truth. Thankfulness is easier for me
when I get outside of my own little world.

I'm not especially fond of rain. I think my folks could have been
much sterner with me about my lack of thankfulness for rain when
I was a child. I'm not happy to admit it, but I grew up loathing
the rain and made no effort to hide my sentiments. In fact,
I still don't jump for joy when the skies cloud over.

But moving to a new climate has greatly helped my outlook.
We no longer live in an area where the forecast of rain automatically
means a long, gray winter complete with days and days of
indoor recess, rubber boots, and raincoats. Here in the Midwest,
rain arrives in the spring and summer and helps the crops to grow.

I'm not especially fond of rain. I think my folks could have been much sterner with me about my lack of thankfulness for rain when I was a child. I'm not happy to admit it, but I grew up loathing the rain and made no effort to hide my sentiments. In fact, I still don't jump for joy when the skies cloud over.

I've been blessed to personally know farmers who are very thankful for those drops that fall from the sky, no matter how many picnics the wet weather may spoil.

A friend of mine once told me that she never prayed for rain. She knew that whenever it rained, some folks wanted it and some folks didn't. Marlyce, who was married to a farmer for almost 36 years, was happy to leave the condition of the skies to God. Wisely, she was thankful for His choice in the matter.

Thankfulness is easier for me when I get outside of my own little world.

My friend Debi lives in Africa. She sleeps under mosquito netting and does not have a bathroom in her house.

We have more than enough bathrooms in our home and most of the time our window screens keep the bugs outside. It would be a challenge for me to live as Debi does, but she would never want me to feel sorry for her. She loves her job and the friends she's made. I'm too swift to complain, at least mentally, if the bathroom is occupied or if a mosquito bothers us in the night.

Debi does not get regular mail service, not the type I'm accustomed to receiving. It often takes months for her packages to arrive. Letters do not take quite as long, but it can't compare to how easy we have it in the United States.

Have you ever waited impatiently for something to come in the mail? I have. Many times. But I was not separated from my family and friends. I had ease of life while I waited, although I may have argued that at the time. The temptation to complain about rising costs and service is ever upon us. If I'm wise, I'll hold my tongue and remember Debi, who has reminded me that God is in control.

Thankfulness is easier for me when I get outside of my own little world.

My world expanded again after we'd lived in the Midwest for a few years. On this occasion we took a little trip north—not too many hours away, but up into the heart of paper mill country. In this region it's common to see mountains of logs stacked very high, and you cannot miss the strong smell that the process creates. We all complained about that smell, and I probably complained the most. But my friend Norma, who lives in the area, had this to say: *It's the smell of jobs, Lori. Don't ever forget that.*

Thankfulness is easier for me when I get outside of my own little world.

It's taken years to see that I needed to get out of my own little world in order to be thankful. It didn't happen overnight, but it did happen.

While working on this book, I came across an allegorical story I had titled "The Boat." As I read through it, I was pleased to realize that I have since become more thankful. But I also found it interesting that, from time to time, God still pulls me out of my settled world and comfortable life in order to get my attention.

Thankfulness is easier

for me when I get

outside of my own

little world.

The Boat

I have a great boat. Someone else looking at my boat might not be too impressed, but I think it's a great boat. I know I spend too much time in my boat, but I feel so safe in it that I just can't seem to help myself. I have a hard time dealing with certain things when I'm outside the boat, so I just find it easier not to leave it at all.

My boat has a comfortable seat; well, it could be better, but I get along okay. The boat is fairly long and the sides are quite high, well, maybe a little too high—sometimes I miss things. But the wood is fairly new, although it could use a new coat of paint. In fact, I've had a few compliments on my boat. Some people think I've got it rather nice.

There is one problem with my boat, but it's a problem I don't like to think about. God doesn't like my boat. He calls it a faithless boat. I've tried to tell Him that's not true and that if He would send people to my boat, I would minister to them. But He always gently tells me that I must come out of the boat and trust Him before I can be of use.

Life went on like this quite some time with me staying in the boat and God calling me out. Then I got a great idea—I'd spruce up my boat!

I got right to work. I painted all the woodwork and padded the seat. I even sent away for a large umbrella in case it rained.

I was very excited to show the Lord. But He didn't share my joy. He smiled at me in His gentle way and said something about men noticing the appearance of the boat, but He was more concerned with hearts.

I was rather angry with God after that. After all the time and money I had put into my boat, He still wanted me to climb out of it. I anchored my boat in shallow water and fumed. God just didn't understand how it was with me and my boat. We had been together for a long time, and when I was in my boat I didn't need to worry about anyone but me.

I didn't ask the Lord to visit me in my boat for some time after that. I was terribly lonely for His fellowship, but forced myself not to call Him. Time went by—too much time. The paint on my boat started to fade and peel and chip, and some stuffing started to come out of my seat cover. My umbrella blew away in a wind storm.

Finally, I was so lonesome I just knew I had to invite God to my boat. He surprised me by coming immediately, as though He had no other plans. As usual, He stood beside the boat to speak to me. I was again surprised to find He wasn't angry with me for not calling Him for so long. His look was as loving and tender as it had always been.

It was the look on His face that finally changed me, the way His eyes filled with love as He extended His hand the way He'd done so many times before and said, "Take My hand and step out of the boat."

This time I did. And together, hand in hand, we walked on the water and up onto the shore, where we stood together and looked out to sea. I watched an unexpected wave take my boat far out to meet the horizon. I knew I would never see it again.

The moment of panic that came over me diminished when I felt His hand squeeze mine ever so slightly. I looked up into the love-filled eyes of my Savior, and all doubts disappeared. As we walked along the shore, He told me how He was going to use me in great and mighty ways, now that I was finally out of my boat.

"Come, follow me," Jesus said,

"and I will make you fishers of men."

MATTHEW 4:19 NIV